FIGHTERS DEFENDING THE REICH

The clean lines of the Bf 109G–2 can be clearly seen in this profile view of an aircraft of 4/JG 54 on the Eastern Front (398/1767/22).

FIGHTERS DEFENDING THE REICH

Bryan Philpott

A selection of German wartime photographs
from the Bundesarchiv, Koblenz

Patrick Stephens

First published 1978 in World War 2 Photo
Albums series
Second edition 1988

British Library Cataloguing in Publication Data

Fighters defending the Reich : a selection
  of German wartime photographs from the
  Bundesarchiv, Koblenz.—2nd ed.
  1. Germany. Air operations by Germany.
  Luftwaffe. 1939–1945. Illustrations
  I. Philpott, Bryan, *1936 –*
  940.54'21

  ISBN 1-85260-156-6

Cover illustrations
Front A rare colour picture of a Bf 109 of I/JG 2
at dispersal (via Jerry Scutts).
Back The armoured windscreen and method of
canopy opening are illustrated by this
photograph of a Bf 110 (658/6395/6A).

*Patrick Stephens Limited is part of the
Thorsons Publishing Group, Wellingborough,
Northamptonshire, NN8 2RQ, England.*

Printed in Great Britain by
Adlard & Son Limited,
Letchworth, Hertfordshire

10 9 8 7 6 5 4 3 2 1

CONTENTS

CAMPAIGN MAP 6

AUTHOR'S INTRODUCTION 7

ABOUT THE PHOTOGRAPHS 13

THE PHOTOGRAPHS 14

APPENDICES 93

Acknowledgements
The author and publisher would like to express their sincere thanks to Dr Matthias Haupt and Herr Meinrad Nilges of the Bundesarchiv for their assistance, without which this book would have been impossible.

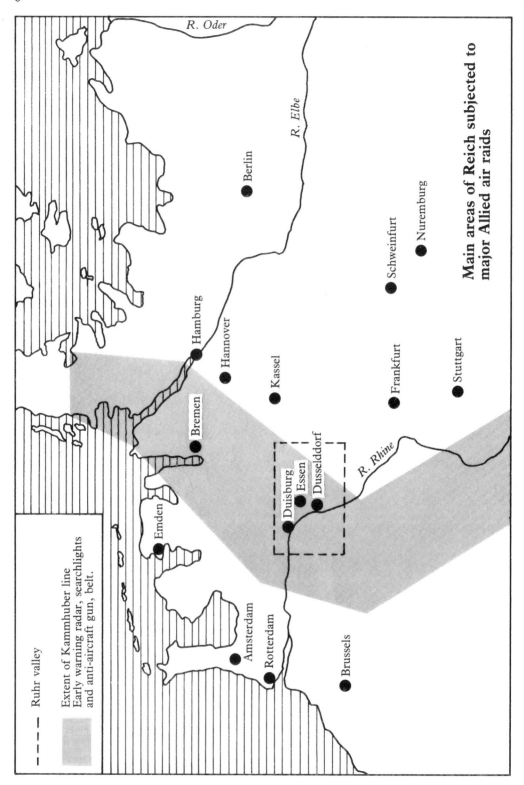

Main areas of Reich subjected to major Allied air raids

R. Oder

R. Elbe

R. Rhine

Berlin

Nuremburg

Schweinfurt

Hamburg

Hannover

Frankfurt

Kassel

Stuttgart

Bremen

Duisburg
Essen
Dusseldorf

Emden

Amsterdam

Rotterdam

Brussels

--- Ruhr valley

Extent of Kammhuber line
Early warning radar, searchlights
and anti-aircraft gun, belt.

When Germany invaded Poland on September 1 1939, the Luftwaffe had a strength of over 4,200 aircraft and looked to be superior to any other air force in the world. But in many ways its strength was illusory, for it had few reserves and a number of its bomber and fighter units were below their planned numerical establishment. During the previous year the overall rise in operational strength had been about 25 per cent, the majority of this being attributable to the increase in supply of transport aircraft, dive bombers and reconnaissance machines. This seems to indicate that Göring clearly saw the coming air war as one in which the Luftwaffe would operate mainly in a tactical support role, both in terms of providing a means of clearing the way for the army, as well as maintaining supplies from the air once air and ground superiority had been achieved.

His failure to expand fighter units to the same extent as the rest of the Luftwaffe had been since its official unveiling in March 1935 appears to indicate that he felt his bombers would not need fighter protection in depth, and there was no major requirement for them in defending the German homeland. The defence of Germany was in the hands of a few day fighters, which were considered to be adequate to counter any enemy bombers foolish enough to enter German air space, and a considerable number of anti-aircraft guns supported by searchlights for use in the unlikely event of air raids occurring at night.

Göring's belief that the air forces against which his own Luftwaffe would be matched were incapable of mounting a successful bomber offensive is underlined by his often misquoted remark made during a July 1939 tour of Rhineland defences: 'If an enemy bomber reaches German soil, my name is not Hermann Göring. You can call me Meier.' It must be remembered, however, that at this time he had no idea that Germany would be faced with a war of the proportions it was to reach within two years.

Nonetheless, it is hard to reconcile Göring's opinions which, on the one hand indicated that enemy bombers would not penetrate German air space, and on the other that there was no defence against the bomber, a view he is known to have shared with other air leaders of the time. The most likely explanation is that his own philosophy as far as air war was concerned was that aircraft were intended for use in offensive and not defensive roles, and that the war Germany was about to embark upon would be of short duration. He was also well aware that a high proportion of the forces available to him would be called upon to support Hitler's ground strategies, thus reducing any air defence potential he might consider necessary.

In June 1939 Göring and Hitler had attended a demonstration of radar at the Luftwaffe technical development centre at Rechlin, which impressed them sufficiently to authorise the purchase of 800 Würzburgs and 200 Freyas. However, there is little indication that the full implication of early warning radar was fully appreciated. In fact, Göring left the study of its strategic importance to his signals chief, General Martini, who was unable to assess successfully the growth of parallel British developments and use of such equipment. So in 1939 there were no priority plans to equip the Third Reich with any form of early warning radar system, although Ernst Udet did persuade Göring to experiment with a small force of single-engined fighters in the night fighter role. But the latter was not viewed by Göring as being of any great importance, for when General Jeschonnek, the Luftwaffe Chief of Staff, raised the matter at a meeting on September 5 1939 he was told that night fighting would never happen.

During the opening weeks of the war the RAF made several attacks on shipping at sea and German naval bases at Wilhelmshaven and Brunsbüttel, achieving little material damage but losing several Wellington and Hampden bombers to defending fighters. One of the most significant raids took place on December 18 1939 when a large force of Wellingtons was decimated by Bf 109s and Bf 110s of I/ZG 76 from Jever, II/ZG 77 from Wangerooge, III/ZG 77 from Nordholz, and 10/JG 26 from Jever.

On this occasion the German fighters were

given advance warning via Freya radar operated by the Luftwaffe and Navy. Although communication between the radar controllers and the fighter squadrons was not all that it might have been, the result was a lesson which seems to have gone unnoticed by the Luftwaffe high command since no immediate action was taken to install similar early warning radar systems along all the approaches to Germany. During the winter of 1939–40, British bombers regularly penetrated German air space carrying out reconnaissance and dropping leaflets as well as the odd few tons of bombs, but there was little damage to the German mainland. Similarly, the bombers more often than not escaped the attention of the much-vaunted Luftwaffe Flak regiments as well as the few fighters which managed to take off to intercept them.

Göring now realised that anti-aircraft guns and searchlights were not an adequate deterrent to night bombing, so he summoned Hauptmann Wolfgang Falck, the commander of I/ZG 1, who had been using his Bf 110s since April as night fighters, to Wassenaar and appointed him the commander of the first Luftwaffe night fighter Geschwader. Four weeks later, on June 18 1940, Colonel Josef Kammhuber was made commandant of the first night fighter division, which at this time comprised Falck's newly formed Geschwader with just two Gruppen: I/NJG 1 under Hauptmann Radusch and Major Blumensaat's III/NJG 1 which had been formed from IV/JG 2 and had just converted from the Bf 109 to the twin-engined Bf 110. Kammhuber's night fighter force consisted of less than 50 aircraft, but by the end of 1940 it had grown to over 150 and was in the throes of becoming a well-organised and efficient fighting unit. The major problem facing the new night fighter commander was devising a method of effecting interceptions with the equipment currently available. This would then help him to achieve his first aim which was the defence in a restricted zone of the German western frontier.

Kammhuber also intended to use his night fighter force in long-range intruder operations harassing the bombers as they returned to their home bases. His first priority, however, was to help the fighter pilots find their target, and to do this he gave immediate attention to the installation of a belt of searchlights and sound locators astride the route usually followed by British bombers. The obvious counter-measure of simply avoiding this belt gradually saw it extended until it covered the whole approach to the Ruhr.

At this time Kammhuber knew little about radar, but General Martini assigned six trained signal companies to him and they, with their Würzburg equipment, evolved a system known as *Helle Nachtjagd* (illuminated night fighting). This method was based on the use of two Würzburg radars; one controlled a master searchlight and the other tracked the movements of the night fighters, which operated within a defined sector. Messages were passed to the fighter crews by R/T and they relied on being vectored into a position where visual contact with the enemy bomber could be made while it was still illuminated by the searchlight.

Kammhuber's next move was to set up ground-controlled radar stations at 20-mile intervals along a line from Schleswig Holstein to Liège. Each of these stations was equipped with a Freya radar for area surveillance and two Würzburg radars for precision location; one to track the individual bomber and the other the night fighter. Information from the two precision sets was plotted on to a table where it was interpreted by a fighter control officer who vectored the night fighter into a position behind the selected target from where a visual interception was carried out. This method was code-named Himmelbett and was the foundation on which all future night fighter ground control was based.

Apart from problems in devising a method of ground control, Kammhuber also had two other difficulties, one was the supply of aircraft and the other suitable crews.

The first aircraft assigned to the night fighter squadrons were Bf 110s, Ju 88s and Do 217s, none of which were designed for such a role. Later specialised versions of the Bf 110 and Ju 88 were to become the backbone of an extremely efficient night fighter force, but in 1940 the former was virtually a heavy escort fighter and the latter a modified bomber.

At the time the night defence of the Reich was beginning to present problems to which rapid answers were necessary, the German Army and Luftwaffe looked to be sweeping all before them; Poland, the Low Countries and France had fallen, and only the RAF and the Channel stood in the way of total victory. It is easy to understand, therefore, why experienced crews who had fought through these campaigns were upset when they were moved from the front to form the nucleus of a night fighter force, just as victory seemed to be theirs. Veteran crews were essential as night flying was an acquired skill. Indeed, those who had combat experience were the obvious choice, since they were also well versed in handling the twin-engined fighters which were to form the backbone of what became the Luftwaffe's fastest growing arm.

At this early stage of the war it is interesting to reflect that Göring was having to call on existing combat units to develop the air defence of the Reich, indicating that he had no real depth in reserves of either aircraft or crews. Fighters had not received a very high production priority, a situation that was to prevail until it was far too late. When they did become available in quantity in late 1944, there were insufficient trained pilots to fly them, nor enough fuel to maintain an effective level of operations. But in 1940 this was all a long way off and Göring was confident that the fighter squadrons at his disposal were sufficiently mobile to be moved into areas where threats were materialising by day, while the newly forming night fighter squadrons could provide a protective umbrella at night.

Göring's proposed strategy was coloured by the fact that the Luftwaffe was not planned to be a defensive force, and that a long drawn out war was very unlikely. He also felt that diversionary campaigns on other fronts would last only a few weeks, therefore enabling him to move his fighter squadrons to any area they were needed for defence rather than in support of the army. Hitler's influence over Göring must not be overlooked; on many occasions the Führer reversed decisions made by his Commander-in-Chief which had initially been made with sound tactical thinking.

A notable example of Göring's authority being undermined occurred during October 1940 when Kammhuber was forming his night fighter force. One of the proposals put to Göring was the use of modified Ju 88 and Do 217 bombers in the intruder role to attack British night bombers as they took off or returned to their bases. Göring was enthusiastic about this plan and gave Kammhuber the go-ahead to encompass it within his night fighter force, using some 40 aircraft. When Hitler heard of the plan he was horrified to think of bombers being used as fighters and immediately reduced the proposed intruder force by half.

The intruder force was always a thorn in Hitler's side. He continued to interfere with policy and on several occasions vetoed Kammhuber's plans, eventually ordering Göring to disband the units in August 1943 when the RAF night blitz was at its peak; a time when such operations may well have paid dividends. During the winter nights of 1940–41 the embryo night fighter force was learning its trade against RAF bombers which were not really working to any effective plan or strategy. One of the earliest victories by a Bf 110 from a *bona fide* night fighter squadron, I/NJG 1, fell to Leutnant Werner Streib and his radio operator Unteroffizier Lingen on the night of July 20 1940 when they destroyed a Whitley. Streib went on to become a very successful first generation night fighter pilot and after his seventh victory – three coming in the space of one 40-minute sortie – he was promoted Hauptmann and given command of I/NJG 1.

Pilots like Streib, Ehle, Griese, Förster and Blumensaat did not have sophisticated radar aids as did their successors, but they were instrumental in getting the new force off on a sound footing as well as bringing it some much-needed publicity which would help to attract suitable recruits from other units who still viewed night fighting with some scepticism.

There was no such jaundiced view from the day fighter pilots in France. Throughout the summer months of 1940 they had been fighting the RAF in the skies over the Channel and England in an offensive rather than defensive role. But as 1941 progressed they were to enjoy changes in equipment as well as tactics. In June 1941 the Germans mounted 'Operation Barbarossa', the invasion of the Soviet Union, and to do this had removed most of their fighter squadrons from the Western Front. The only units left in France to combat the increasing daylight intruder operations of the RAF were JG 2 under the command of Hauptmann Wilhelm Balthasar, and JG 26 under Oberstleutnant Adolf Galland. The various elements of these two Geschwader were fairly well dispersed along the Channel coast and in France, although the 7th Staffel of III/JG 26 was detached to the Mediterranean. Numerically they totalled about 150 aircraft which, at the time of the major Luftwaffe withdrawal to the east in June, were all sub-types of the Bf 109, the latest being the Bf 109F which had entered service with JG 51 earlier in the year.

In July the RAF increased its activity in an effort to relieve the pressure on the Russian front by having Luftwaffe units returned to the west, but the two Jagdgeschwadern in France proved more than capable of meeting the increased threat, finding few problems against the obsolete Blenheims which formed the bulk of the daylight bomber offensive. Escorting Spitfires, and occasionally Hurricanes, often tangled with the Bf 109s, but the German fighter pilots were now operating with all the advantages the RAF had had the previous year. The Bf 109s were flown by experienced pilots led by experts, and despite their numerical inferiority inflicted an average loss rate of 2:1 during the two years they fought their campaign. In August 1941 the two Luftwaffe units involved accounted for 108 RAF fighters for the loss of 18 of their own number.

Such a rate of attrition could not be withstood by the RAF who in November 1941 called a halt to their offensive operations to conserve their strength for a refreshed spring onslaught. Hopes of success with new aircraft such as the Boston escorted by Spitfire Vs were still-born, since the Luftwaffe also had a new fighter which the RAF had only briefly encountered in late 1941 – the superlative Focke-Wulf FW 190. As is often the case with successful aircraft, the FW 190 did not receive favourable initial reaction from the pilots of II/JG 26 who started to receive the Focke-Wulf in July 1941. The 'Butcher Bird', as it became known, was criticised for its lack of firepower and more than one pilot requested a return to the Bf 109F–4. Gradually the problems were ironed out and, although combats in the autumn had not proved conclusive one way or the other, the new fighter had achieved its first success and was growing in popularity.

The ascendancy gained by the FW 190, which can be said to have started in the defence of the *Gneisenau*, *Scharnhorst* and *Prince Eugen* during the Channel dash on February 12 1942, continued to such a degree that JG 2 and JG 26 spent more time on offensive sorties than they did in defending their colleagues against the sporadic RAF bomber raids. The RAF offensive was carried out by twin-engined light bombers which without a fighter escort were no match for the Bf 109s or FW 190s. The Focke-Wulf also proved a tough opponent for the Spitfire V, and it was not until the gradual introduc-

tion of the Spitfire IX towards the end of the year that the tide began to turn once more.

The pattern outlined in France applied equally in Holland and other enemy-occupied countries, where comparatively few Luftwaffe fighters were able successfully to combat intrusions of their air space. By mid-1942 the Germans had set up a chain of early warning radar stretching from Leeuwarden to Brest – primarily at the instigation of Kammhuber for his night fighter force – and these were able to give the fighter pilots plenty of prior warning of the build-up of RAF raids.

Freya radar could detect bomber formations at a range of about 56 miles if the aircraft were above 1,000 feet. As the RAF had used a policy of forming up in spiralling climbs to 5,000–7,000 feet before setting course, the intention of practically every raid was known to the German controllers. Diversionary sweeps and feints were used in attempts to foil the radar operators, but most of them were very experienced and not easily fooled. The end result was that they were able to assemble their FW 190s and Bf 109s in good time and place them in a position where they had height and sun advantage. The Luftwaffe fighter pilots involved in these operations were all very experienced, most of them having fought throughout the Battle of Britain and other campaigns. As the Luftwaffe had no policy of resting pilots after a tour of duty (they simply had four weeks' annual leave), individual scores could mount to astonishing proportions. But of more serious consequence in the long term was that veterans were being killed when their expertise at training schools would have been welcomed. In March 1942 these skilled pilots accounted for 32 RAF fighters, and in the following month losses rose to a staggering 104, these successes being due to the early warning radar system and the FW 190.

Morale was very high, with both air and ground crews enjoying a good standard of living, with very few shortages in equipment which in itself was of excellent quality. Many fighter pilots were now wearing full leather flying clothing, comprising separate black leather trousers and flight jackets, and the old-fashioned Kapok-filled life jacket had given way to a slim-line inflatable version.

However, in August 1942 there appeared on the horizon a new shape and another air force, which in the long run was to make a large contribution to the defeat of Germany.

The new shape was the massed boxed formations of B–17 and B–24 bombers, and the air force was the United States Army Air Force, which had been arriving in strength in England since America declared war on Germany. On August 17 1942 12 B–17Es of the 97th Bombardment Group, 8th Air Force, led by General Ira C. Eaker, attacked marshalling yards at Rouen-Sotteville to open the planned daylight bomber offensive. On this occasion the US bombers were well escorted by Spitfires and returned to England without loss. But the RAF had warned their American cousins of the hazards of daylight bombing, for they had not attempted any further deep penetrations by heavy bombers since April 17 1942 when 12 Lancasters of No 44 Squadron had been decimated during an attack on the MAN engine works at Augsburg. On the occasion of the first USAAF raid the German fighter pilots had been unable to penetrate the fighter screen and had not worked out the best methods of attack to be used against massed bomber formations. However, two days later the Jagdgruppen pilots were able to underline their efficiency when they took a heavy toll of RAF aircraft during the Dieppe landings. During the course of the day-long running battle, which was the largest single air engagement in World War 2, the RAF lost 106 aircraft, 88 of which were fighters, against the Luftwaffe's loss of 48. The heaviest-hit unit was I/JG 2 which lost eight FW 190s; other Gruppen of JG 2 and JG 26 suffered losses of experienced pilots but replacements and aircraft were still readily available.

On September 6 1942 FW 190s of II/JG 26, led by Hauptmann Egon Meyer, penetrated the Flying Fortresses' defensive screen and Meyer destroyed a 97th BG B–17F, the first to fall to an FW 190 in France.

By November 1942 the American bombers had ventured further afield and embarked on their first strategic campaign. At the same time the German fighter pilots hit upon the idea of mounting head-on attacks against the mass formations. Attacks from the rear and sides met very heavy defensive fire but, by sweeping ahead of the box formations, then climbing above to turn and dive head-on, such fire was more than halved. Closing speeds rose to over 500 mph so the fighter pilots only had a brief moment to pick their spot, aim and fire, but the heavy-calibre weapons of the FW 190 proved adequate for even the briefest encounter. American losses were not astronomical and by no means deterred them, but in the opening months of 1943 the first daylight raids against German targets were made and ominous signs began to appear. Day fighters were joined by Bf 110s of the night fighter force, the first eight from II/NJG 1 going into action on February 4 1943, and they began to take a mounting toll of the four-engined bombers.

Every effort was made to strengthen the forces defending the Reich and units which had been moved to the eastern and Mediterranean fronts were recalled to Germany. The pendulum gradually swung against the American bombers and, although in June P–47 Thunderbolts started to escort them, they still became fairly easy prey once the P–47's range forced the fighters to turn back. In October, the 8th Air Force suffered its most crippling loss when 60 B–17s failed to return from Schweinfurt and well over 100 more received serious damage. The FW 190s, Bf 109s, Ju 88s, Bf 110s and Me 410s had a field day once the escorting fighters had left the bombers, and added to the mounting bomber losses which, since July, had been causing grave concern.

However, in many ways it was the beginning of the end for the now hard-pressed fighter squadrons trying to defend their homeland. Hitler continued to interfere with Luftwaffe policy and by now Göring was a spent force, drugs having reduced his ability to comprehend even the simplest strategy, or even believe the facts presented to him by his commanders. When Galland reported to him after the October Schweinfurt raid, that P–47s had escorted the bombers as far as Aachen and proof existed in the form of a shot-down American fighter, Göring refused to believe him and claimed that the pilot must have glided to Aachen after his machine had been damaged. The fitting of improved long-range tanks to the P–47s, the introduction of the P–51, and the twin-engined P–38, all tipped the scales back in favour of the attackers. Throughout 1944, daylight raids increased in intensity and, although German fighter production rose from around 1,000 aircraft per month in July 1943 to a staggering 2,995 per month in September 1944, lack of trained pilots and, towards the end of 1944 and early 1945, a serious shortage of fuel, just added to the problems. New weapons in the form of air-to-air missiles fired into the Fortress formations, a few rocket-powered interceptors, and some jet fighters all brought brief hope to the Luftwaffe. But the veterans who still survived knew there was no hope, and the courage displayed by youngsters with just a few flying hours in their log books was not any form of insurance against the highly trained and well-equipped Allied air force.

As the day fighters fought a withdrawing battle across the Continent, the night fighter Gruppen were faced with similar moments of glory interspersed with frustration.

Since the build-up of Kammhuber's night fighter force in 1941 the techniques of airborne interception at night and in bad weather had gradually been improved and perfected. In the summer of 1941 airborne radar carried in the Do 217s, Bf 110s and Ju 88s had been introduced and, although this met some opposition at first, due to a marginal loss of speed, its advantages were soon appreciated. Those who at first eyed it with suspicion, among them being Hauptmann Helmut Lent, one of the first night fighter aces, were converted.

The night fighters took a steady toll of RAF bombers and by mid-1943 over 95 per cent of the force then operating was fitted with airborne radar which greatly increased the chances of interception once the ground stations had vectored the fighter into the bomber stream. During the onslaught by Bomber Command in 1943, measures and counter-measures by both sides tilted the scales one way then the other. Jamming of both ground and air radar forced the Luftwaffe into introducing free-range night fighters operating in what was known as *Wilde Sau* roles. Most of these aircraft were single-seaters, usually Bf 109s or FW 190s, which patrolled in the area of the bomber stream and relied on the pilot's eyesight, aided by flares and searchlights, to locate the bombers. The *Zahme Sau* type of operation was the one most favoured by crews and brought greater success. In this the twin-engined long-duration fighters were free from ground control and could roam outside their designated sectors. Quite often the ground stations would initially direct the aircraft towards the incoming bomber stream, then the radar operator on board would take over. Interceptions might start to occur way out over the North Sea, during the approach to the target, or even when the bomber turned for home. The long duration of the fighters and their heavy firepower, which in 1943 included the introduction of vertically firing 30 mm cannon known as *Schräge Musik*, generally gave the edge to the defenders. The night fighters' war developed into one where radar and radio aids played a major role. From 1944 until the end of hostilities these devices were developed to a high degree by both sides and laid the foundations of modern electronic warfare.

Despite losses inflicted by the night fighters and ground defences, there were only rare occasions when they were above an acceptable rate to Bomber Command, one of these being on the night of March 30 1944 when 94 bombers from a force of 795 attacking Nuremburg were shot down. Deep penetrations by the RAF were curtailed partly because of the losses inflicted by the night fighters, but mainly due to a switch from strategic targets to tactical ones.

The growing assault by the RAF and USAAF on oil refineries, lines of communication, railway systems and similar objectives contributed to the steady decline in Luftwaffe operations. Eventually a serious shortage of fuel, lack of pilots, and the Allied advance which overan the ground radar stations negated the night fighter force in the same way that the day fighters were also to suffer. The latter continued to put up spirited opposition right to the end, on some occasions flying jet fighters from autobahns, but by May 1945 they had to admit defeat at the hands of a powerful allied air force, which by this time was superior in almost every respect.

Luftwaffe fighter pilots fought gallantly to defend their homeland, but hindsight now shows that indifferent leadership, too great a dispersion of forces, and a lack of fighter production until it was too late, all combined to stack the odds too greatly against them.

Author's note: As mentioned in 'About the photographs', the Bundesarchiv photographic records are not complete, so it has not been possible to include a selection of late night fighter photographs. In view of this, the text has been slanted towards the early years of the defence of the Reich.

ABOUT THE PHOTOGRAPHS

The photographs in this book have been selected with care from the Bundesarchiv, Koblenz (the approximate German equivalent of the US National Archives or the British Public Records Office). Particular attention has been devoted to choosing photographs which will be fresh to the majority of readers, although it is inevitable that one or two may be familiar. Other than this, the author's prime concern has been to choose good-quality photographs which illustrate the type of detail that enthusiasts and modellers require. In certain instances quality has, to a degree, been sacrificed in order to include a particularly interesting photograph. For the most part, however, the quality speaks for itself.

The Bundesarchiv files hold some one million black and white negatives of Wehrmacht and Luftwaffe subjects, including 150,000 on the Kriegsmarine, some 20,000 glass negatives from the inter-war period and several hundred colour photographs. Sheer numbers is one of the problems which makes the compilation of a book such as this difficult. Other difficulties include the fact that, in the vast majority of cases, the negatives have not been printed so the researcher is forced to look through box after box of 35 mm contact strips – some 250 boxes containing an average of over 5,000 pictures each, plus folders containing a further 115,000 contact prints of the Waffen-SS; moreover, cataloguing and indexing the negatives is neither an easy nor a short task, with the result that, at the present time, Luftwaffe and Wehrmacht subjects as well as entirely separate theatres of operations are intermingled in the same files.

There is a simple explanation for this confusion. The Bundesarchiv photographs were taken by war correspondents attached to German military units, and the negatives were originally stored in the Reich Propaganda Ministry in Berlin. Towards the close of World War 2, all the photographs – then numbering some $3\frac{1}{2}$ million – were ordered to be destroyed. One man in the Ministry, a Herr Evers, realised that they should be preserved for posterity and, acting entirely unofficially and on his own initiative, commandeered the first available suitable transport – two refrigerated fish trucks – loaded the negatives into them, and set out for safety. Unfortunately, one of the trucks disappeared en route and, to this day, nobody knows what happened to it. The remainder were captured by the Americans and shipped to Washington, where they remained for 20 years before the majority were returned to the government of West Germany. A large number, however, still reside in Washington. Thus the Bundesarchiv files are incomplete, with infuriating gaps for any researcher. Specifically, they end in the autumn of 1944, after Arnhem, and thus record none of the drama of the closing months of the war.

The photographs are currently housed in a modern office block in Koblenz, overlooking the River Mosel. The priceless negatives are stored in the basement, and there are strict security checks on anyone seeking admission to the Bildarchiv (Photo Archive). Regrettably, and the author has been asked to stress this point, the archives are *only open to bona fide authors and publishers, and prints can only be supplied for reproduction in a book or magazine.* They CANNOT be supplied to private collectors or enthusiasts for personal use, so *please* – don't write to the Bundesarchiv or the publishers of this book asking for copy prints, because they cannot be provided. The well-equipped photo laboratory at the Bundesarchiv is only capable of handling some 80 to 100 prints per day because each is printed individually under strictly controlled conditions – another reason for the fine quality of the photographs but also a contributory factor in the above legislation.

THE PHOTOGRAPHS

FW 190A–3 of II/JG 1 in France in 1942. The *Tatzelwurm* on the cowling is red edged with black, and the spinner has a white spiral on a black/green background. The *Tatzelwurm* was first used by JG 3 and was often painted in Staffel colours (361/2193/32).

Left Bf 110G–4 undergoes engine tests ready for the coming night's work (492/3346/13).

Close-up of *Tatzelwurm* marking and wheel detail on another JG 1 FW 190A–3 (361/2193/26).

Bf 110G–2 of NJG 200. The leading aircraft is coded 8V + IN and is a II Gruppe machine. The individual aircraft letter 'I' is red outlined in white (502/198/24).

FW 190A–3 of Geschwader Stab JG 26. This aircraft was flown by the 1A officer Hauptmann Rolf Hermichen and carries a personalised form of the first two letters of his surname (604/1528/17).

Safe from prying eyes. A Bf 110G–4 night fighter concealed from roving Allied reconnaissance aircraft (492/3346/27).

Bf 109F–4 of the Luftwaffe ace Hans 'Assi' Hahn of III/JG 2, France 1941 (602/7235/39A).

Two pilots, possibly of II/JG26, at readiness in front of their Bf 109Fs. The pilot on the right is wearing a flight jacket carrying the insignia of a Oberfeldwebel and the one on the left is holding a 'Victory Stick', which was a form of fighter pilot's trophy on which aerial victories were logged by cutting notches (597/540/1).

A 21 cm rocket loaded in place in its launching tube beneath the wing of the FW 190A–8/R6 featured in the photograph on the right (674/7772/28A).

This is an interesting shot of a III/JG 2 Bf 109F being reloaded at Caen in 1941. The rubber mat to protect the wing, the flap arrangement, aileron mass balance and wing root paint scheme are all of use to the modeller (602/7235/34A).

A Geschwader Stab FW 190A–8/R6 of JG 26 being loaded with a W Gr 21 rocket. This aircraft has another variation of the spiral spinner decoration favoured by Luftwaffe pilots (674/7772/16A).

Inset left Bf 109G–10/U4 Wrk No 413555 approaches to land with everything hanging. Of note is the tall wooden rudder and Galland clear-type hood. The fuselage cross is in grey (677/8004/28).

Inset right Bf 109G–5 of a Jagdfliegerschule (fighter pilot school) indicated by the four-letter code and number under the canopy (661/6605/30A).

Background photograph Two more Bf 110E night fighters, this time from 7/NJG 4 photographed in 1941. Colours as previous photograph (360/2095/30).

A II Gruppe FW 190A–4 of an unknown unit in France 1943. The camouflage is typical of the period and the '5' on the aircraft in the background is a good example of the variety of styles to be seen (377/2814/18A).

A II/JG 2 FW 190A–4 at readiness. The ground crew display a diverse selection of dress while the pilot appears to envy them their meal. The stylised paint scheme behind the exhaust stacks was a feature of many FW 190s, especially those flown by JG 2 (482/2854/25A).

A Bf 109 G–10 moves on to a temporary taxi-way in 1945. The camouflage is 74/75/76 with heavy mottled fuselage and splinter wings and tail units (464/382/6A).

Early style night fighter camouflage. This Bf 110E of NJG 1 is painted black overall and has grey codes. The individual aircraft letter 'B' is red outlined in white. This aircraft carried no AI radar and had comparatively weak offensive armament which can be seen in the nose. The *Englandblitz* badge of the night fighter arm was painted on both sides of the nose (594/297/33A).

Left This is the Bf 109G–5 of Oberfeldwebel Heinrich Bartels of IV/JG 27. The aircraft is Red 13 and although used in the Mediterranean theatre is included as it gives an excellent detail view of the inboard flaps and engine cowlings (526/2306/37).

Right Interesting detail view of the underwing MG 151 gondola on the Bf 109G–5 shown on the left (526/2306/37).

Below right Hauptmann Gerhard Barkhorn's Bf 109G–5 of II/JG 52. Photographed on the Eastern Front, it shows good detail of 74/75/76 camouflage, Gruppe Commander's chevron and aircraft's name. These features can all be seen on many Luftwaffe fighters irrespective of theatre of operations (649/5355/21).

Below This photograph illustrates the poor view from the cockpit of the FW 190, as well as the familiar spiral spinner and engine cooling fan (463/351/15).

Above Luftwaffe pilots used a variety of methods to record aerial victories. Oberfeldwebel Josef Kociok uses his 'Victory Stick' to point out the kill markings on the tail of his Bf 110F of 10(NJ)/ZG 1. The stick carries the same symbols as the aircraft, the 12 white bands indicating day victories and the 8 black, night victories. The crew man on the right is an Unteroffizer (641/4544/21A).

Left Roundels for RAF and stars for USAAF victories on the rudder of this FW 190A of Josef Wurmheller, the Staffel Kapitan of 9/JG 2. The pilot is wearing a Luftwaffe officer's flight blouse which is blue/grey in colour (483/2895/32).

Below left Date of victory and nationality of victim, in this case all RAF, on the port rudder of Leopold Fellerer's Bf 110G–4 of II/NJG 5 (660/6553/21). **Below right** Simple vertical bars record the successes of Hauptmann Walter Krupinski, Staffel Kapitan of 7/JG 52. Aircraft is a Bf 109G (613/2326/26).

Inset above The scattered remains of a USAAF B–17 shot down by fighters in 1943 (637/4155/35).

Background photograph A P–51D of the 334th FS, 4th FG, 8th USAAF which failed to return from an escort mission over Germany in 1944 (497/3525A/20).

Inset right Luftwaffe personnel remove the waist gun from B–24J 27586 of the 703rd BS, 445th BG, 8th USAAF. This aircraft had a black F in a white disc on the fin; its letter was Q+ and on its nose, in addition to 11 mission marks, it carried the legend 'God Bless our Ship' (665/6834/9A).

A Lancaster bomber shot down by night fighters on October 19 1942 (*unnumbered print*).

Low-level beat-up by Leutnant Woidisch of I/JG 52 (498/39/31).

FW 190A–8 of II/JG 26 is manhandled into its dispersal area among the trees. Camouflage is 74/75/76 and the picture was taken in France in early 1944 (493/3352/28)

Modellers who strive for true authenticity might like to follow the example of these civilian workers, by using their air brushes to spray German national markings (638/4222/12).

A B–24 awaits transportation to a scrapheap where it will be broken down into useful components to be used by the German aircraft industry (490/3251/9).

Above A Bf 109G–14 taxies out at Merzhausen during the latter days of the war. The aircraft has the vertical identifying band of III Gruppe behind the fuselage cross, but its unit is not known (495/3429/8).

Above left German troops appear to be using the tail unit of this 8th Air Force B–17 as a rest haven. Close examination reveals four apparently taking refreshment under the tail, while the others look to be engrossed in some form of demonstration. Note the rifles stacked near the tail (637/4135/6A).

Left Mail from home. A mechanic working on the engine of a Ju 88 night fighter takes a welcome break to read a letter from home. The lipped engine cowling and radar aerials are of interest as are the white spinners with black spirals – a reverse of the usual practice (678/3144/16A).

Above right and right Modellers of large-scale aircraft should find these photographs of the so called 'Galland' hood particularly useful (680/8264/14 and 674/7777/17A).

Above The lethal 30 mm *Schräge Musik* cannon set at a 70° angle can be clearly seen in the rear cockpit of this Bf 110G–4. What appears to be a black disc on the engine cowling is, in fact, the exhaust system (492/3346/11).

Above right Trainee fighter pilots have the defensive cones of fire of the B–24 demonstrated to them. The instructor is obviously making the point that a head-on attack is the best ploy to use when trying to shoot down the heavily armed American bomber (565/1406/29).

Right A No 1 Squadron Typhoon on a Luftwaffe scrapheap. The aircraft suffered engine failure on December 22 1943 whilst being flown by Warrant Officer J. Wyatt, an Australian flying with the unit, during an attack on V1 sites. (488/3079/5).

Left A fighter pilot of JG 3 sits astride a 66-gallon centre-line tank in front of his Bf 109G in which he has just shot down a B–17. The date was October 30 1943 (76/124/5A).

The Heinkel He 219A-2 was one of the finest night fighters to come out of World War 2. This aircraft was the machine flown by Obersleutnant Werner Streib (65 night kills). If it had been available in greater quantity it would have taken a very heavy toll of RAF night bombers. The aircraft illustrated is fitted with SN 2 radar. The He 219 was also fitted with ejection seats (72/4/32).

Luftwaffe mechanics and ground crew were often called 'Black Men' because of their one-piece working overalls. The two on the left are wearing these while the man on the right seems to have acquired a white pair, or perhaps they even had that well-known washing powder in Germany! Boxes on the right are ammunition containers (667/7102/19A).

Single-seat fighters were adapted for the night fighter role and used on *Wilde Sau* operations. This FW 190A–6/R11, Wrk No 550143, was flown by Oberleutnant Fritze Krause of I NJGr 10. Camouflage is 74/75/76 and the badge on the nose is the boar's head of JG 300. The aircraft is equipped with FuG 217 radar. The original negative in the Bundesarchiv is captioned FW 190A–9/R11, but it is believed that only four of this version were built and did not enter service. Although the author has been shown a photograph from a private collection which was also marked as an A9 version, all the evidence suggests that the aircraft concerned could not have been A9 versions of the FW 190. However, it is still interesting to ponder on how two photographs in different locations have similar captions (74/123/31).

The standard rear defensive armament of the Bf 110 – two 7·9 mm machine-guns (663/6740/23).

Background photograph Searchlights turn night into day over a German city (595/317/23A).

Inset top A standard German searchlight being demonstrated to a Japanese delegation in early 1942 (673/7673/16).

Inset left A Luftwaffe-controlled searchlight (701/384/11).

Inset right Women undertook tasks to free men for more strenuous work, as they did in both the British and American armed forces (674/7757/31).

Left Part of a night fighter control centre with the staff preparing for the coming night's work (355/1798/39).

Right Luftwaffe female clerk prepares her plotting equipment. This and other photographs indicate a certain slackness of dress under the open tunic which is most uncharacteristic of the German nation (658/6359/16).

Far right and below right Two views of a Würzburg radar installation. The scanner is on a Fu MG 62 which had a range of 56 miles (621/2830/28 and 331/3346/17).

Below Civilian plotters in a control centre. The girls used the torch-like apparatus to pinpoint the plots on a large-scale map (633/3818/7A).

Above Oberstleutnant Josef Priller and his FW 190A–7 of JG 26 in June 1944. This aircraft has a mottled rudder and not yellow as often depicted in drawings of Priller's aircraft. The yellow rudder was painted on another of Priller's machines, part of which is shown in the photograph on the left. The different style '3' and the personal markings can be clearly seen (298/1753/15 and 493/3352/12).

Right Oberstleutnant Priller preparing for a sortie. He is wearing a leather flight jacket over which is a late-style inflatable life jacket (490/3274/7).

Starboard view of Priller's FW 190A–7 shown in the photograph at the top of page 42 (490/3274/12).

Reloading the 13 mm MG 131 machine-guns of a Bf 109G–6. Each gun carried 300 rounds (666/6893/14).

A useful detail shot for modellers of a Bf 109G–10/U4 (674/7774/25).

Kill markings were not the prerogative of fighter pilots. The scanner of this Würzburg radar tracking station lists aircraft by type and date of destruction (662/6660/24A).

Top Two Bf 110Gs of NJG 6 with early type FuG 202 Lichtenstein BC radar aerials on the nose (659/6436/15).

Above Bf 110G–2 of NJG 6 (659/6436/12).

Left A Major of the night fighter force has his safety harness adjusted by an Oberfeldwebel, who is possibly his radar operator (492/3342/37A).

Above right The peculiar-looking camouflage on the top surfaces of this FW 190A–6 of II/JG 26 is, in fact, a shadow cast by the camouflage netting under which it is concealed (482/2864/16A).

Right Bf 109G–6/R6 of II/JG 26 in France in 1942. The wing leading edge slots are extended, and the barrel of the port underwing MG 151 cannon can be clearly seen. These points, plus the unusual paint scheme at the wing root, make this a very useful and detailed source of reference (487/3066/7).

Inset above No good fighter pilot should be without his signal pistol and flares shown here strapped to the leg for easy access. The cylinder at the waist is for inflating the life jacket (613/2333/22A).

Inset below W Fr Gr 21, 21 cm rocket tube from which mortar shells were launched at massed USAAF formations can be seen under the wing of a Bf 109G–6/R2. The badge to the rear and below the cockpit refers to part of the aircraft's internal equipment (650/5445/6).

Background photograph and inset below The two photos here do not depict an aircraft from the European theatre but have been included because they are very good shots of a Bf 109G–5. In this case the aircraft belongs to the 7th Staffel of III/JG 27 and was photographed in 1943. The rudder and tail band are white (529/2383/20 and 529/2383/21).

The codes under the port wing of this Bf 109G–5 Trop would seem to indicate that it is awaiting ferrying to an operational unit. The aircraft in the background, which can be more clearly seen in the photograph below, does not have a tropical filter, but oddly enough carries the badge of JG 27, a unit associated with the Middle East campaign. These aircraft were probably at a unit equivalent to an RAF MU (658/6394/30 and 658/6394/28A).

This line-up of Bf 109Gs is interesting in that the aircraft appear to have the Defence of the Reich bands painted around their tails. It is likely that the machines concerned belonged to JG 27 which used a dark green band on their Bf 109s (662/6658/8A).

Bf 109G–10/U4 of the 7th Staffel of III/JG 3. Camouflage is 74/75/76 and the aircraft's rudder is white (674/776/20A).

The poor forward view from the cockpit of the FW 190 often meant that one of the ground crew guided the pilot by lying on the wing and using hand signals. This aircraft is an FW 190G–8 of I/SKG 10 at Dreux (496/3493/21).

Servicing engines in winter conditions was made slightly more comfortable by the provision of a small tent. Here one is used for an FW 190G–3, photographed in Romania in 1943 (500/101/23A).

Bf 109G–6s of the Hungarian 102 independent fighter group serving with the Luftwaffe in the summer of 1944 (503/241/5A).

Bf 110G–2 of an unknown unit carrying long-range underwing tanks. The Oberleutnant has a zipped flight jacket with fur collar and standard issue flying boots (662/6658/17A).

Left A Bf 110G–2/R3 with a belly gun pack containing a pair of MG 151 cannon. August 1943 (502/198/21).

Facing page Crews gather beside their Bf 110G–2s of ZG 1 prior to taking off for attacks against USAAF day bombers during the summer of 1943. The aircraft have white fuselage bands, black/white spiral spinners, and the code 2N is one-fifth the size of the normal identification letters (676/7975/11 and 676/7975/10).

Below This Bf 110G night fighter, an early mark G–2 belonging to NJG 200, which operated only in Russia, is fitted with flame dampers but no radar. It has a belly pack which contained two MG 151 cannon. The *Englandblitz* badge of the night fighter arm can be clearly seen against the grey camouflage (658/6360/7).

Bf 109Gs of JG 27 with underwing cannon gondolas, and a centre-line fuel tank rack. The diced spinner of the leading aircraft shows another variation of Luftwaffe decoration (658/6394/16).

The twin 7·9 mm MG 17 machine-guns mounted in the upper cowling of this FW 190 A–3 receive their ammunition from a 'black man' (464/381/21).

FW 190A–3 of 7th Staffel III/JG 3 'Richthofen' in France 1942. The pristine finish of the aircraft is marred only by the exhaust stains which illustrate why JG 3 later adopted a decorative bird motif in this area (604/1542/21A).

Yet another style of spiral adorns the spinners of this Bf 110G–2 of ZG 1 (676/7975/7).

Above Two *Rotten* of FW 190s and Bf 110s scramble to intercept a daylight raid (502/198/29).

Above right A Bf 110G day fighter of II/ZG 1 returns from a sortie (502/198/6).

Right Even a war does not prevent the niceties of civilisation, as proved by these Luftwaffe pilots who seem to be enjoying their meal in the summer sunshine. Those at readiness are wearing a variety of flying clothing ranging from shirt sleeves to leather jackets and lightweight flight jackets. The aircraft are probably from III/JG 3 (613/2316/22A).

Left An FW 190 pilot ruefully examines the damage to his aircraft's starboard wing, caused by B–17 gunners. France, 1943 (325/2776/5).

Background photograph A *Schwarme* of II/ZG 76 Bf 110s peel off to reveal their under fuselage gun packs, rocket tubes and drop tanks (663/6734/22A).

Inset below 5th Staffel Bf 110Gs of ZG 76 at low level. These aircraft caused problems to the American daylight bombers until long-range close escort by P–47s and P–51s made operations too hazardous for them (663/6737/34).

Inset right Hauptmann Heinz Strüning (56 kills) of NJG 1 and 2 in the cockpit of his Bf 110G-4. He was awarded the Oakleaves to his Ritterkreuz on 20 July 1944, and was killed in action on 12 December 1944. The *Englandblitz* badge of the night fighter force and the heavily armoured windscreen, are worth noting (658/6354/7).

Right Two mechanics (right) talk with two aircrew on the wing of a Bf 110. All four men are wearing the popular Luftwaffe Képi-style cap. The steel helmet packed with the bundle to the left is an aircrew type often worn by bomber crews. The step and aerial beneath the wing root provide useful modelling detail. The barrels to the right of the mechanic are not *Schräge Musik* (502/198/27).

Left This photograph shows very useful detail of the armoured windscreen and method of canopy opening on the Bf 110. The Bf 109Gs are possibly from I/JG 27 (658/6395/6A).

Below left 21 cm rockets being loaded aboard the twin tubes of a Bf 110G–2 day fighter of 7/ZG 26, while Staffelkapitän Hauptmann Kiel watches (649/5371/15).

Below Plenty of atmosphere in this photograph of a Bf 109G–5 being rearmed. The centre-line tank is of 66 Imperial gallon capacity (650/5439/20).

64

Above left This Luftwaffe Major appears to be undergoing some form of test since the officer to his right is a Leutnant of the medical branch as shown by his collar patch. The badge beneath the Major's collar patch looks to be a unit device, but even under very great magnification cannot be identified positively (342/631/29). **Above right** FW 190A in the landing pattern (502/198/19). **Below** Bf 110G–2/R3/U9 with four 21 cm rocket tubes, long-range tanks and twin-gun underbelly armament pod (663/6739/27).

Bf 109G–10 of III/JG 3. The pilot to the left has an Iron Cross First Class beside his pilot's badge and also has a form of qualification badge above his left pocket. Both men wear the standard Luftwaffe eagle on their right breast. The two styles of flight jacket are also of interest (666/6894/10A).

Removed engine cowlings, long-range tanks, and twin rocket tubes make this a useful reference photo of a Bf 110G from II/ZG 76. Nose armament and cowling have been removed completely (663/6736/18).

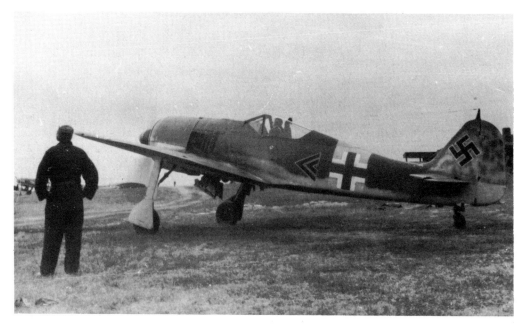

Above An FW 190 of a Jabo unit with empty fuselage and bomb racks. The pilot's parachute rests on the tailplane, an insurance against any effects damp grass might have if it has to be used (502/194/13).

Right Single 21 cm rocket tube installed under the port wing of a Bf 110F of an unknown unit (658/6385/17).

Above left A very pleasing shot of the Gruppe Commander's FW 190A of I Gruppe. The aircraft is from an unidentified unit, and the photo was possibly taken on the Eastern Front (664/6789/262).

Left Oberfeldwebel, with Knight's Cross at neck, life jacket under arm, heavyweight flying suit and standard flight jacket, awaits orders to take his already bombed-up FW 190 on a ground-attack sortie. Oil streaks and exhaust stains make useful modelling guides (500/121/3).

Right Bf 109G–14, possibly of JG 53 in early 1945 (674/7775/30A).

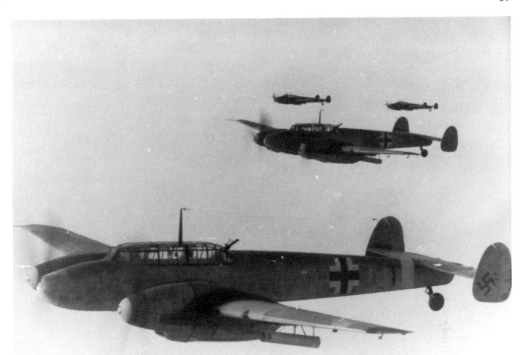

Above Bf 110Gs from III/ZG 26 on an interception mission. These aircraft have yet another style of spinner decoration (649/5370/41).

Above left FW 190A–7 in a spring-like setting. The small '9' forward of the cross is unusual. The aircraft seems to be taxiing towards its hide among the trees (494/3400/6).

Left This FW 190A–3 is on a temporary taxi strip made from railway sleepers. The large '2' on the fuselage is of conventional size and worth comparing with the markings in the previous photo. The aircraft individual number is repeated on the wheel covers (375/2721/14).

Right The tail-up attitude, huge baulks of wood before the wheels, and the mechanics adjusting the guns indicate that this FW 190 is in the firing butts (630/3586/5A).

The camera has stopped the propeller blades of this FW 190A–4 just after the point of touch down. The spray from the wheels indicates that the aircraft is still moving at some speed (459/144/19).

Left This FW 190A–4 has a unique mix of camouflage styles. The top fuselage decking is a form of splinter, the rudder has odd streaks and the under cowling is mottled. This is a I Gruppe aircraft of an unidentified unit (489/3168/20).

Inset This photograph shows the FW 190's fuelling point, but in this case it would appear that fuel is being drained, or the second pipe is acting as a overflow valve. The mat protecting the wing surface is also noteworthy. The aircraft shown is FW 190A–3 of JG 2 (597/512/16).

Mechanic guides pilot of FW 190 of II/SG 2. The empty bomb racks indicate a successful ground-attack sortie (500/104/14A).

Right Pilots of JG 2 confer by the tail of one of their aircraft. The wire seeming to hang below the wing is a whip aerial for the FuG 16Zy Morane equipment (497/3525/14).

Below right Gruppe Adjutant's damaged Bf 109G–2 of II Gruppe (unidentified unit). The cowling camouflage does not match the rest of the aircraft and could indicate that this component has been 'borrowed' from another aircraft (614/2430/33).

Left and below These two photos are of considerable interest as they show a photographer with a cine camera inside the fuselage of an FW 190. The low-level pass clearly shows the photographer filming from the removed panel. The pilot is wearing a throat microphone which was quite common among Luftwaffe fighter pilots and the aircraft is A–4 of JG 2 (492/3345/17 and 492/3345/25).

Inset left FW190A–4/U3 with armoured cowling ring and white/black spinner. Probably on the Eastern Front (500/106/15).

Inset above Bf 109G–6 of JG 104, a Jagdschule training fighter pilots in 1944. The three-figure codes before the cross indicate a training school (676/7975/29).

Background photograph Two ground crew snatch a quick nap in what could be almost termed the original bunk-bed sequence. The aircraft is a Bf 109G–6 (503/239/7).

Above and above right Unusual camouflage on these Bf 109 G–6s and G–14s of a Luftwaffe fighter pilots' school in mid-1944 (676/7974/13 and 676/7974/9).

Right Pilots, displaying a wide variety of flying clothing, discuss their flight plan. The pilot on the left has a 'Victory Stick' in his hand, and an older-style flying suit than the one on the right. The extended foot rest and parachute placed on the tail are worth noting (502/193/32A).

Left Bf 109G–6 of JG 27 whose badge can be seen on the removed engine cowling under the port wing (662/6656/38A).

Trainee fighter pilots at Jagdschule JG 104 in 1944. At this time, pilot training had been severely curtailed and youngsters with only just over 100 hours were being thrown into the front line (676/7975/32).

Right Although only parts of aircraft are visible, the photo reveals a mass of useful information. The swastika on the centre machine has no white edge; the camouflage pattern on the top fuselage decking is rather unusual; and the wing in the foreground clearly shows that the splinter camouflage does not have a hard edge (489/3169/11A).

The ammunition tanks of a JG 54 Grünherz Bf 109F–4 being filled while an instrument mechanic checks the cockpit. Another Eastern Front aircraft, but a lot of useful detail which applies to any Bf 109 (385/1533/10A).

Inset The combination of leather trousers, fleece-lined boots and a rather odd-looking webbing belt around his flight jacket does not somehow convey the sartorial elegance normally associated with fighter pilots (498/39/28).

Bf 109F of II/JG 51. This is the aircraft of the Luftwaffe's top ace Hauptmann Erich Hartmann, most of whose victories were obtained on the Russian Front (607/1821/5).

Bf 109G of 15/JG 52, a Croatian volunteer unit (498/42/10A).

Three pilots from a squadron of Croatian volunteers serving with JG 52 on the Eastern Front. The man in the centre is a Feldwebel and wears a mission clasp under his Luftwaffe breast badge; the one to the right is an Unteroffizier, but the rank of the third man is obscured by his flight jacket and life jacket. The aircraft is a Bf 109G–6 and carries the Croatian arms (498/41/34A).

Bf 109G pilot making final pre-flight checks. The mottle camouflage and loop aerial are useful modelling details (499/74/6).

This Bf 109F pilot is wearing Luftwaffe Tuchrock breeches and unlined leather boots. The aircraft has a very light mottle camouflage which gives it the appearance of one colour overall. A previous owner's Gruppe marking has been painted out behind the fuselage cross (499/57/11).

Above Like all air forces, the Luftwaffe could only operate with full support from its ground crew, who in so many publications are overlooked. This line-up in front of a Bf 110G–2 has uniformity only in headdress (676/7973/28).

Above right The guns of a Bf 109G–6 are harmonised in the firing butts. Note the ammunition boxes being used to support the jacks under the wings. (658/6394/26A).

Right Stencil markings are very much in evidence on this Bf 109G–6 whose pilot could well be recalling a recent victory. The odd shape on the cowling is the shadow of the propeller blade (650/5439/14).

Left Pilot of a reconnaissance Bf 110F discusses his sortie as cameras are loaded into his aircraft. It carries simplified wing and fuselage crosses (496/3453/17).

The handle protruding from the cowling of this Bf 109G–6 was used to start the DB 605 AM 12-cylinder engine. The chevron markings of a Gruppe Commander can just be seen to the rear of the cockpit (649/5381/31).

Conditions such as this thick clinging mud made life difficult for air and ground crews on all fronts. This Bf 109G–6 of II/JG 3 has its cover removed as the pilot (right) prepares to carry out his pre-flight external checks (634/3890/8).

The Croatian pilot of this Bf 109G–6 of 15/JG 52 has accomplished a successful wheels-up landing causing only superficial damage to his aircraft (498/42/20A).

All air forces have their pin-ups. These girls are taking a break from a physical training lesson at a Luftwaffe school. Women served in clerical, medical, mechanical, parachute packing and cooking roles (447/1968/30).

Left Late-style inflatable life jacket, zippered flying suit and elasticated cuffs to the flight jacket indicate the high standard of equipment being used by Luftwaffe aircrew. Aircraft is a late G-type Bf 109 and carries a III Gruppe symbol behind the simplified fuselage cross (674/7774/17).

Right Seventeen kill markings on the tail of C9 + EN flown by Wilhelm Johnen which landed at Dübbendorf on 28 April 1944 where the photograph was taken. The last kill marking is dated 15 2 44. (*Swiss Air Force Museum via Bundesarchiv*).

Below This Bf 110G–4/R1, Wrk No 5547, of 6/NJG 6 landed at Dübendorf on March 15 1944 and was later returned to the Luftwaffe. It was equipped with four 7·9 mm machine-guns and two 20 mm cannon (*Swiss Air Force Museum via Bundesarchiv*).

Inset It seems as though the Unteroffizier in the centre has just received promotion, as the jacket over his arm carries the insignia of a Feldwebel. If the assumption is correct, he has jumped two ranks as Unterfeldwebel would have been the next logical progression (676/7973/32A).

Background photograph Bf 109F–4 of 7/JG 54, photographed on the Russian Front, carries typical Luftwaffe markings. The white '5' before the fuselage cross is the aircraft's number within the Staffel, while the Gruppe marking after the cross is the old-style Gruppe III insignia later replaced by a verical bar. The heart under the cockpit is the Grünherz of JG 54, and the badge below the cockpit is of the III Gruppe. The aircraft has standard national insignia and four black victory bars on its recently damaged rudder.

Another shot of Wilhelm Johnen's Bf 110G-4/R3 C9 + EN of 5/NJG 5 which landed in neutral Switzerland on April 28 1944. The radar is FuG 212 and FuG 220, and the aircraft had no guns in two of its nose positions but carried 20 mm cannon in the other, as well as 30 mm *Schräge Musik (Swiss Air Force Museum via Bundesarchiv)*.

The aerials of the FuG 202 radar on Bf 110G–4 of 6/NJG 6 which defected to Switzerland on March 15 1944. The photograph was taken at Dübendorf in Switzerland. The same picture has appeared in many publications on the Luftwaffe purporting to have been taken at a variety of Luftwaffe night fighter bases *(Swiss Air Force Museum via Bundesarchiv)*.

1. Day and night fighter units and their aircraft, June 1944

JG 1   Stab, I and II Gruppen – FW 190A–8. III Gruppe – Bf 109G–10.

JG 3   Stab, I, II and III Gruppen – Bf 109G various sub-types. IV Gruppe – FW 190A–8.

JG 5   I and II Gruppen – Bf 109G–10.

JG 11   Stab and 10/JG 11 – Bf 109 and FW 190. I and III Gruppen – FW 190A–8. II Gruppe – Bf 109G–6.

JG 27   Stab, I, III and IV Gruppen – Bf 109G various sub-types.

JG 53   II Gruppe – Bf 109G–14.

JG 54   III Gruppe – FW 190A–8.

Einsatz JGr 104, 106, 108 – Bf 109G–5.

JG 2   Stab and I Gruppe – Bf 109G–10.

JG 26   Stab and I Gruppe – FW 190A–8. III Gruppe – Bf 109G–10.

ZG 1   II Gruppe – Me 410B–2.

ZG 26   Stab, I and II Gruppe – Me 410. 7/ZG 26 – Bf 110G–2.

JG 300 Stab – FW 190A–6. I, II and III Gruppen – Bf 109G–6.

JG 301 I Gruppe – Bf 109G–6.

JG 302 I Gruppe – Bf 109G–6.

NJG 1   Stab and I Gruppe – He 219 and Bf 110G–4. II and III Gruppen – Bf 110G–4. IV Gruppe – Bf 110G–4 and Ju 88G–1.

NJG 2   Stab, I, II and III Gruppen – Ju 88G–1.

NJG 3   Stab and I Gruppe – Ju 88 G–1, Ju 88C–6 and Bf 110G–4. II and IV Gruppen Ju 88C–6. III Gruppe – Bf 110G–4.

NJG 4   Stab – Ju 88G–1. I Gruppe – Ju 88C–6 and Bf 110G–4. II and III Gruppen – Do 217N–2 and Bf 110G–4.

NJG 5   Stab, I, II, III and IV Gruppen – Bf 110G–4.

NJG 6   Stab, I and III Gruppen – Bf 110G–4.

NJGr 10 He 219A–5, Bf 110G–4 and Bf 109G–6/U4N.

I/NJG 7 Ju 88G–1.

---

2. Fighters used by the Luftwaffe in the defence of the Reich

DAY FIGHTERS comprised most versions of the Bf 109 and FW 190. The following are typical examples:

Messerschmitt Bf 109G–6

Span: 32 feet $6\frac{1}{2}$ inches. Length: 29 feet 7 inches.
Engine: DB 605A–1 12-cylinder, liquid-cooled, inverted V.
Performance: Maximum speed 387 mph, service ceiling 39,750 feet.
Armament: Two 13 mm MG 131 machine-guns with 300 rpg, one 20 mm MG 151 cannon with 150 rounds, and two 20 mm MG 151 cannon in underwing gondolas with 120 rpg.

Focke-Wulf FW 190A–8

Span: 34 feet $5\frac{1}{2}$ inches. Length: 29 feet.
Engine: BMW 801D 14-cylinder, air-cooled radial.
Performance: Maximum speed 408 mph, service ceiling 37,400 feet.
Armament: Two 13 mm MG 131 machine-guns and four 20 mm MG 151 cannon.

NIGHT FIGHTERS

Messerschmitt Bf 110G–4b/R3

Span: 53 feet $4\frac{3}{4}$ inches. Length: 41 feet $6\frac{3}{4}$ inches.
Engines: Two DB 605B 12-cylinder, liquid-cooled, inverted V.
Performance: Maximum speed 342 mph, service ceiling 26,000 feet.
Armament: Two 30 mm MK 108 cannon with 135 rpg, two 20 mm MG 151 cannon with a total of 650 rounds, and two 7·9 mm MG 81 machine-guns in rear cockpit.

Junkers Ju 88G–7b

Span:	65 feet 7½ inches. Length: 51 feet 1½ inches.
Engines:	Two Junkers Jumo 213E–1 12-cylinder, liquid-cooled, inverted V.
Performance:	Maximum speed 363 mph, service ceiling 32,810 feet.
Armament:	Four 20 mm MG 151 cannon with 200 rpg, two MG 151 cannon firing obliquely upwards with 200 rpg, and one 13 mm MG 131 machine-gun with 500 rounds.

Dornier 217N–2

Span:	62 feet 4 inches. Length: 58 feet 9 inches.
Engines:	Two DB 603A 12-cylinder, liquid-cooled, inverted V.
Performance:	Maximum speed 320 mph, service ceiling 29,200 feet.
Armament:	Four 20 mm MG 151 cannon and four 7·9 mm MG 17 machine-guns.

Heinkel 219A–7/R1

Span:	60 feet 8½ inches. Length: 50 feet 11¾ inches.
Engines:	Two DB 603G 12-cylinder, liquid-cooled, inverted V.
Performance:	Maximum speed 416 mph, service ceiling 41,600 feet.
Armament:	Two 30 mm MK 108 cannon in wing roots, two 30 mm MK 103 cannon and two 20 mm MG 151 cannon in ventral tray, and two 30 mm MK 108 cannon firing obliquely upwards.

3. Luftwaffe fighter pilots with more than 150 victories to their credit

	Score	Units
Major Erich Hartmann	352	JG 52
Major Gerhard Barkhorn	301	JG 52, 6, 44
Major Günther Rall	275	JG 52, 11, 300
Oberleutnant Otto Kittel	267	JG 54
Major Walter Nowotny	258	JG 54, 7
Major Wilhelm Batz	242	JG 52
Major Theo Weissenberger	238	JG 5, 7
Major Erich Rudorffer	222	JG 2, 54, 7
Oberstleutnant Heinrich Bär	220	JG 51, 77, 1, 3
Major Heinz Ehrler	220	JG 77, 5
Oberstleutnant Hans Philipp	213	JG 54, 1
Leutnant Walter Schuck	206	JG 5, 7
Oberleutnant Anton Hafner	204	JG 51
Hauptmann Helmut Lippert	203	JG 52
Oberst Hermann Graf	202	JG 52, 53
Hauptmann Walter Krupinski	197	JG 55, 11, 26, 44, 51
Major Anton Hackl	190	JG 11, 26, 300
Hauptmann Joachim Brendle	189	JG 53, 51
Hauptmann Max Stotz	189	JG 54
Hauptmann Joachim Kirschner	185	JG 3, 27
Hauptmann Werner Brändle	180	JG 3
Leutnant Günther Josten	178	JG 52
Oberstleutnant Joh Steinhoff	176	JG 52, 77, 7, 44
Hauptmann Günther Schack	174	JG 51
Hauptmann Heinz Schmidt	173	JG 52
Hauptmann Emil Lang	173	JG 52, 53, 26
Oberleutnant Ernst Reinert	169	JG 27, 77, 7
Major Horst Adameit	166	JG 54
Oberst Wolf Wilcke	161	JG 53, 3
General Major Gordon Gollob	160	JG 3, 77
Hauptmann Hans Joachim Marseille	158	JG 51, 27
Oberleutnant Gerhard Thyben	157	JG 3, 54
Oberleutnant Hans Beisswenger	152	JG 54
Leutnant Peter Düttmann	152	JG 52

Other titles in this series

Panzers in the desert
by Bruce Quarrie

German bombers over England
by Bryan Philpott

Waffen SS in Russia
by Bruce Quarrie